The Top and Bottom of the World

By Allan Fowler

Consultants

Linda Cornwell, Learning Resource Consultant,
Indiana Department of Education

Fay Robinson, Child Development Specialist

Lynne Kepler, Educational Consultant

Children's Press®
A Division of Grolier Publishing
New York London Hong Kong Sydney
Danbury, Connecticut

Project Editor: Downing Publishing Services
Designer: Herman Adler Design Group
Photo Researcher: Caroline Anderson

Library of Congress Cataloging-in-Publication Data

Fowler, Allan.
The top and bottom of the world / by Allan Fowler.
p. cm. – (Rookie read-about science)
Includes index.
Summary: Describes the location, climate, and animal life of the cold regions at either end of the earth.
ISBN 0-516-20321-5 (lib.bdg.) 0-516-26160-6 (pbk.)
1. Polar regions—Juvenile literature. [l. Polar regions.] I. Title. II. Series
G590.F68 1997 96-28767
998–dc20 CIP
AC

Printed in the United States of America.
3 4 5 6 7 8 9 10 R 06 05 04 03 02 01

Try this. Hold a small ball in one hand — with one finger on the top and your thumb at the bottom.

Now imagine your ball is planet Earth.

Then each of these spots would be one of Earth's poles, the North Pole or the South Pole.

The region around the North Pole is called the Arctic.

The region around the South Pole is called the Antarctic.

Both regions are always very cold.

And both are “lands of the midnight sun.”

Summer lasts six months near the poles — and the sun can be seen in the sky all day and all night.

Winter lasts the other six months — and it's always dark.

You can't see the sun at all.

When it's summer at the North Pole, it's winter at the South Pole.

The North Pole is in the middle of an ocean — the Arctic Ocean.

The South Pole is in the middle of land — a mountainous continent called Antarctica.

Much of the Arctic Ocean is thick ice that never melts. Nobody lives on that ice.

But a few hardy people live in the cold lands touched by the Arctic Ocean.

The Inuit of Canada and Alaska sometimes make houses out of blocks of hard snow. These dome shaped houses are called igloos.

The Laplanders of northern Europe depend on herds of reindeer for food and clothing.

Heavy-coated animals such as Arctic hares, Arctic foxes, and polar bears live in the Arctic lands.

On the shores of Arctic islands, there are many colonies of puffins. These birds dive for fish, which they catch in their big, brightly colored beaks.

Whales, seals, and walruses swim in Arctic waters. Many of them visit Antarctica in the summer, along with some sea birds.

Beluga whales

Kerguelen fur seals

Walruses look much like seals, except they are larger and have tusks.

One bird, the Arctic tern, nests and breeds in the Arctic when it's summer there.

Then, when winter comes, the tern flies all the way to Antarctica — halfway around the world!

The only animals that live all year long in Antarctica are penguins and some tiny insects.

And only a few simple plants, such as mosses, can grow there.

Scientists visit Antarctica to study and explore it, but no people live there.

Except for the mountains, almost all of Antarctica is covered by ice. The ice is as much as three miles thick.

Icebergs are big chunks of Antarctic or Arctic ice that break off and float away in the ocean.

On a summer day in Antarctica, the temperature is likely to be about 0 degrees Fahrenheit.

On a winter day, it might be minus 70 degrees Fahrenheit.

Can you believe that Antarctica was once very warm, and full of vegetation?

It was — long before there were people on Earth.

How much ice is there now in the Antarctic and Arctic regions?

If all of that ice were to melt, the world's oceans would rise nearly 200 feet. Many of the largest cities would be under water!

So let's be glad it stays so cold at the top and bottom of planet Earth.

Words You Know

North Pole (Arctic)

South Pole (Antarctic)

Inuits

Laplanders

icebergs

puffins

penguins

polar bears

whales

seals

Index

About the Author

Allan Fowler is a free-lance writer with a background in advertising. Born in New York, he lives in Chicago now and enjoys traveling.

Photo Credits

©Wolfgang Kaehler — cover, 7, 13, 25, 26, 29, 30 (top right), 30 (bottom left), 31 (top left)

©Ben Klaffke — 3

Tony Stone Images, Inc. — ©Earth Imaging, 4

Valan Photos — ©Fred Bruemmer, 6, 14; ©John Eastcott/YVA Momatiuk, 9; ©Stephen J. Krasemann, 12, 18, 30 (top left), 31 (bottom left); ©Wayne Lankinen, 16, 31 (middle right); ©James M. Richards, 21; ©Joyce Photographics, 24

Alaska Stock Imaages — ©Chris Arend, 10; ©Johnny Johnson, 11, 19, 22, 31 (middle left), 31 (bottom right)

Photo Researchers, Inc. — ©Porterfield/Chickering, 15, 30 (bottom right); ©Stephen Dalton, 17, 31 (top right); ©George Holton/Ocelot, 23

COVER: Icebergs in the Antarctic Peninsula area